BREAKING DOWN PROBLEMS IN COMPUTER SCIENCE

BARBARA M. LINDE

PowerKiDS press
New York

Published in 2019 by The Rosen Publishing Group, Inc.
29 East 21st Street, New York, NY 10010

First Edition

Editor: Jane Katirgis
Book Design: Reann Nye

Photo Credits: Cover Maksim Kabakou/Shutterstock.com; p. 5 SpeedKingz/Shutterstock.com; p. 6 Science & Society Picture Library/SSPL/Getty Images; p. 7 (left) ablephoto/Shutterstock.com; p. 7 (right) Daboost/Shutterstock.com; p. 9 fotoinfot/Shutterstock.com; p. 11 Jacob Lund/Shutterstock.com; p. 13 David Buffngton/Blend Images/Getty Images; p. 14 Brand X Pictures/Stockbyte/Getty Images; p. 15 fizkes/Shutterstock.com; p. 17 michaeljung/Shutterstock.com; p. 18 iinspiration/Shutterstock.com; p. 19 Bloomberg/Getty Images; p. 21 nullplus/Shutterstock.com; p. 23 KK Tan/Shutterstock.com; p. 25 Dragon Images/Shutterstock.com; p. 26 maximino/Shutterstock.com; p. 27 FatCamera/E+/Getty Images; p. 29 https://commons.wikimedia.org/wiki/File:Two_women_operating_ENIAC.gif.

Cataloging-in-Publication Data

Names: Linde, Barbara M.
Title: Breaking Down Problems in Computer Science / Barbara M. Linde.
Description: New York : PowerKids Press, 2019. | Series: Essential Concepts in Computer Science | Includes index.
Identifiers: LCCN ISBN 9781538331323 (pbk.) | ISBN 9781538331316 (library bound) | ISBN 9781538331330 (6 pack)
Subjects: LCSH: Computer science–Juvenile literature. | Computer programming–Juvenile literature.
Classification: LCC QA76.23 L56 2019 | DDC 004–dc23

Manufactured in the United States of America

CPSIA Compliance Information: Batch #CS18PK: For Further Information contact Rosen Publishing, New York, New York at 1-800-237-9932

CONTENTS

TACKLING HARD PROBLEMS

Have you ever planned a party or organized a trip? You've probably written a book report. Perhaps you have played an instrument in a school concert or tried out for a sports team. Did any of these activities seem overwhelming? Did the thought of getting everything done and everyone in the right place at the right time make your head swim?

You're not alone! Many activities that we do are **complex**. They involve a lot of parts, and all of the parts have to fit together just so. Think back to how you worked. You didn't do everything at once. Instead, you broke the activity into smaller tasks. That's what computer scientists do when they face a problem. Read on to find out how they tackle the tough ones.

Planning for an event takes a lot of time and organization. >

COMPUTER SCIENCE BASICS

You probably work with computers now, but did you know that you were involved in computer science? Computer science is the study of computers. A computer scientist uses computers to solve problems.

The computer case, monitor, mouse, and keyboard are called **hardware**. Hardware inside the case includes the fan, hard drive, motherboard, and other small pieces.

ALAN TURING, COMPUTER SCIENTIST
(1912–1954)

Alan Turing was a brilliant British mathematician and one of the first computer scientists. In 1936, he invented a computing machine called the Turing machine. Turing improved on his Turing machine when he designed the Automatic Computing Engine (ACE) in 1945. Machines like this one had memory that could store **programs**. The Turing machine served as the model for the first electronic digital computers.

(Right) The hard drive, motherboard, and other parts of hardware are inside the computer case. (Left) Software powers the apps that are shown in these **icons**.

The term **software** doesn't mean parts that are soft like a marshmallow or a pillow. *Software* refers to the parts that are not hardware. Software is the set of instructions that tell the hardware what to do. System software tells the hardware and other kinds of software how to work together. Application software performs a specific **function**. When computers work together, they use network software.

WHAT IS DECOMPOSITION?

When computer scientists have a problem, such as creating a program or **application**, they use a process called **decomposition**. That means they break the problem down into smaller problems. Each small problem can be examined and solved by itself. When the answers to the small problems are combined, they give the answer to the large, complex problem. Using this process may take some time. However, the result is a program that works well and doesn't have any errors that need to be corrected.

It's also helpful to use decomposition to figure out how an already-existing system works. Suppose you want to understand how a wristwatch works. You could ask an expert to show you all of the parts. Then you could see how each part works separately and together.

COMPUTER CONNECTION

According to Data USA, more than 1.7 million people in the United States work in computer-related jobs. That number keeps growing every year.

8

Computer scientists often collaborate,
or work together, to create programs.

9

WHY IS DECOMPOSITION IMPORTANT?

Computer scientists use decomposition to plan what, when, how, why, and where each part of a process needs to be worked on. They use it to make sure they are giving the correct instructions to the computer. It's also helpful in figuring out the cost.

Decomposition shows how each small part relates to the others and to the final product. Each small part can be given to a different worker or team. Several parts can be worked on at once. This saves time and money.

Computer scientists aren't the only ones who use decomposition. Engineers making a new highway or architects building a skyscraper use it. Your parents use it to cook dinner or plan a trip. If you have written a book report, you have used decomposition, too.

MANY WAYS TO WORK

There are several ways to work with the decomposition process. You can make a list of all of the tasks. People who like pictures or diagrams might create a graphic organizer. Others might write each step on a sticky note and put the notes on a wall or poster board. You might have an entirely different way. Use whatever technique works best for you!

Decomposition helps computer scientists solve hard problems.

11

DECOMPOSE A SANDWICH

Let's use the decomposition process to make a sandwich. Here are the tasks.

Go to the kitchen. Think about the kind of sandwich you want. Make a list of tools, supplies, and actions. Write down every item and action under the correct heading. Then start working. Gather the tools (knife, cutting board, plate). Gather the ingredients (two slices of bread, a jar of peanut butter, a jar of jelly).

Now make the sandwich. Put the bread on the cutting board. Use the knife to put peanut butter on one slice of bread and jelly on the second piece of bread. Put the second slice of bread on top of the first slice. Cut the sandwich in half and put it on the plate. Congratulations! You successfully used the decomposition process.

COMPUTER CONNECTION

You can use decomposition to break down just about any problem. Try it sometime for getting dressed, learning a song, or doing homework.

What tools and supplies do you need to make a peanut butter and jelly sandwich?

OOPS!

Now suppose you left the knife off the tools list. It would be messy to spread peanut butter and jelly with your fingers. So, you'd have to stop and get the knife. You just lost time. Or suppose you put the peanut butter on the bread before you checked to see if you had jelly. If there wasn't any jelly, you might have to stop working and go shopping. You lost time again. Or you could continue, but you would eat a peanut butter without jelly sandwich. What might happen if you skipped a step, like cutting the sandwich in half? In either case, your sandwich would not be exactly the way you wanted it.

14

If you haven't decomposed the problem completely and accurately, you might have errors that need to be corrected.

15

PARTY PLANNING WITH DECOMPOSITION

Let's see how the decomposition process might help you plan a party.

Decompose the problem into smaller tasks, like the following ones. Decide on a date and time. Figure out how long you have to do the planning. Settle on a **budget**. Make your guest list and decide how and when to notify everyone. Find a place to have the party. Think about the refreshments you want to serve. Plan the entertainment, if you are having some. Think about the decorations you want and where you will put them.

What might happen if you left out a task? If you forgot to include decorations, the party could easily go on. But what if you forgot to send out the invitations? All of your work would be wasted.

It's best to write everything down so you can see all of the tasks.

PROGRAMMING LANGUAGES

When you used decomposition for the tasks related to the sandwich and the party, you probably wrote your notes in English. Or you might have used Spanish, Japanese, or another language that you understand.

Computer programmers use special languages to communicate with computers. There are many **programming languages**, including Python and Java.

WHAT'S YOUR LANGUAGE?

NASA, YouTube, and Google all use Python, because it's good for handling information technology, engineering, and design tasks. Java is often used for education, banking, and medical care programs. It also works well for video games. HTML, or hypertext markup language, is used for designing web pages and sending emails.

```c
{
    const char *target_str;
    int target_str_len;
    uint32_t seed = 0;
    int32_t result[1];

    static char *kwlist[] = {

    if (!PyArg_ParseTupleAndK
            &target_str, &target_
        return NULL;
    }
}
```

The languages use a **code** made up of words and numerals combined in a certain way to give instructions to the computer. Programmers are extremely careful and precise when they write code. The code has to be exactly right, or the program won't work. Think about the party again. If you chose the date *May 3* but you typed *May 4* on the invitations, your party would fail.

19

USING ALGORITHMS

If you've ever added, subtracted, multiplied, or divided numbers, then you've used **algorithms**. An algorithm is a set of instructions for doing a task in a sequence and in a set number of steps. A recipe in a cookbook is one example of an algorithm. So is a written list of instructions.

A computer algorithm has to be written in a way that the computer can understand. This involves the use of code and a programming language. The program tells the computer each step to follow. An algorithm tells the program how to correctly follow these steps. It always has a starting point, a list of instructions, and a stopping point.

For your party planning, the algorithm starts with setting the date. It ends when your guests show up at the party.

COMPUTER CONNECTION

Some algorithms have to be done in a certain sequence, or order. For example, an algorithm for baking a cake would direct you to bake the cake in the oven before you iced it.

Computer programmers write algorithms to tell the computer what to do.

21

CREATE A GAME APP

Try using decomposition to create a game app. Here are some questions to ask yourself. Remember to record the answers in a form that you can use.

What kind of game app do you want to make? Do you want a word search or spelling game? Do you want to learn math facts? Maybe you want to build a city or take a trip.

How many characters are there, and what do they look like? Can the user change how the characters look?

Who will play the game? Your audience could be kids your age, or younger ones. You can design for single or multiple players.

What will your app look like? You can choose bright or soft colors, select a busy or calm background, and make other design choices.

IMAGINING APPS

In 1983, Apple co-founder Steve Jobs said that in the future everyone would have "an incredibly great computer in a book that you can carry around with you that you can learn how to use in twenty minutes." By the mid-1990s, apps had been developed that made his vision come true. Today, many people carry smartphones that use apps.

Use your imagination and the decomposition process to design an awesome app.

23

MORE APP PLANNING

What kind of graphics will you use? Will your app have audio? Do you want fast, cheerful music, or other sound effects? You'll need to plan for when the sound is on.

What software will you use? Several types are available. You might need to do some research to find the best one.

How will the user move around in your game? Think about penalties and bonuses for reaching certain goals. Movements, such as hopping and running, might be included.

Who will test your app? Someone who did not help you create the app would make a great tester. You want to make sure that the tester will find any bugs.

Before you start making your app, read through your decomposition process again. Make sure you have everything ready to go.

COMPUTER CONNECTION

Some websites allow you to create an app. Most of them don't require you to know a programming language, so they're easy to use.

Using decomposition can help solve some of your game-making problems.

DR. CLARENCE A. ELLIS

While a teenager in Chicago in 1958, Clarence A. "Skip" Ellis had a job protecting a company's expensive computer. He wasn't allowed to use—or even touch—the computer, but he was so interested in it that he studied the computer manuals and learned all about the machine. He even solved a problem that no one else could.

Ellis studied math and science in college, and he earned a PhD in computer science in 1969. He was

POINT AND CLICK

Before "point and click" became common, a computer operator used the keyboard to type commands. For example, instead of clicking on an icon, the operator would type this: open *C:\filename*. Or a list of text items in the form of a menu would show on the screen and the operator would use the arrow and tab keys to move up and down the menu. Then they would press the "enter" or "return" key to choose a program.

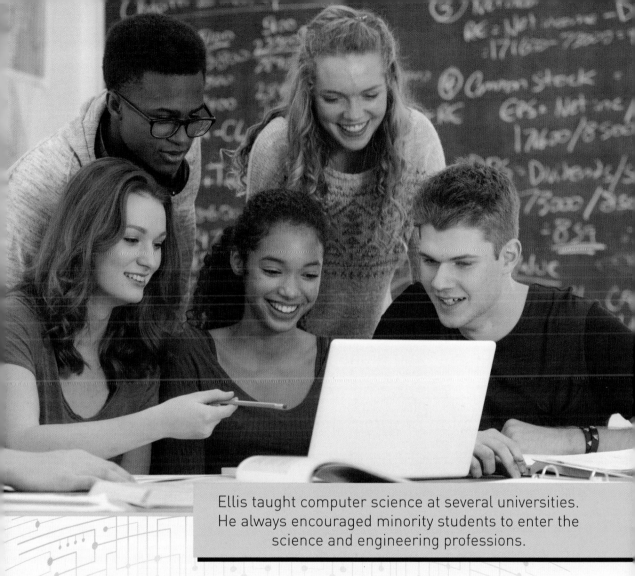

Ellis taught computer science at several universities. He always encouraged minority students to enter the science and engineering professions.

the first African American to receive this degree. He helped develop the technology that lets multiple computer users work on the same document at the same time. He also invented the "point and click" method. Ellis, the first African American computer scientist, received many awards for his work.

BETTY JEAN JENNINGS BARTIK

Betty Jean Jennings Bartik attended a one-room schoolhouse. She studied mathematics in college. She became one of the first computer programmers. Bartik worked with a team of five other women on the ENIAC (Electronic Numerical Integrator and Computer). This was the first electronic digital computer. Bartik was the co-lead on the project. She and the other women taught themselves how to program the computer. Bartik also figured out how to debug errors. Later, she developed hardware and software for other computers. She said about her work: "It was the greatest adventure of my life."

Her college, Northwest Missouri State University, named a computing museum after her. Throughout her life, she encouraged young women to work in science and technology.

COMPUTER CONNECTION

ENIAC operated from 1945 to 1955. At the time, it was the fastest calculating machine in the world. It filled an entire 1,500-square-foot (139 square meter) room.

Bartik was one of the first programmers for ENIAC.

A CAREER IN COMPUTERS

Can you break an everyday problem into small parts? Can you see how parts fit together to make a whole? Can you work hard? Then consider a career in computers.

Start getting ready now. Take plenty of math courses. If your school has computer classes, take them. If not, find someone to teach you, or take some free online classes. Get a four-year college degree in computer science, information technology, or software engineering. If you want to be involved with developing new programs and methods, then stay in school for about four more years to get a PhD.

Computer use is still growing, so the sky's the limit on what you can do with a career in this exciting field.

COMPUTER CONNECTION

Computer programmers make about $80,000 a year. Software application developers make about $100,000. Computer scientists can make more than $115,000.

GLOSSARY

algorithm: A set of steps that are followed in order to solve a mathematical problem or complete a computer process.

application: A program that performs one of the major tasks for which a computer is used. Commonly called an "app."

budget: The amount of money set aside for a project.

code: The lines of text or symbols used to create a computer program.

complex: Not easy to understand or explain; having many parts.

decomposition: The process of breaking something down into smaller pieces.

function: A task that something or someone performs.

hardware: The physical parts of a computer system, such as wires, hard drives, keyboards, and monitors.

icon: A picture on a computer screen that represents a program.

program: A set of code that runs on a computer and performs certain tasks. Also called software.

programming language: A computer language designed to give instructions to a computer.

software: Programs that run on computers and perform certain functions.

INDEX

WEBSITES

Due to the changing nature of Internet links, PowerKids Press has developed an online list of websites related to the subject of this book. This site is updated regularly. Please use this link to access the list: www.powerkidslinks.com/eccs/probs